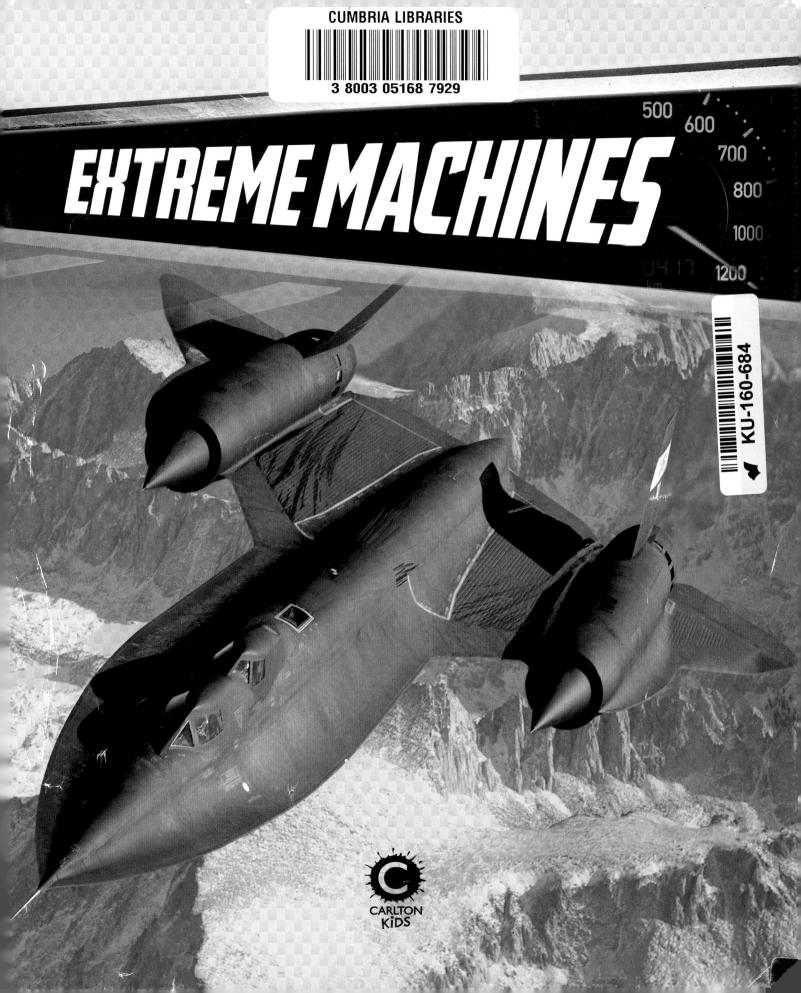

EXTREME MACHINES

500
600
700
800
1000
1200
km

CARLTON KIDS

THIS IS A CARLTON BOOK
Text, design and illustration © Carlton Books Limited 2017, 2019

Author: Anne Rooney
Design and editorial: Tall Tree

First published in 2017
by Carlton Books Limited
An imprint of the Carlton Publishing Group,
20 Mortimer Street, London W1T 3JW
This edition published in 2019

9 8 7 6 5 4 3 2 1

A catalogue record for this book is available from the British Library.

ISBN: 978-1-78312-477-0
Printed in Dubai

CONTENTS

INTRODUCTION 4

TRAVELLING
OVER LAND 6

MOVING THROUGH
THE WATER 26

GETTING OFF
THE GROUND 42

MACHINES THAT
STAY STILL 58

TRAVELLING
ABOUT IN SPACE 70

GLOSSARY 80

EXTREME MACHINES

People have been making machines for thousands of years. Machines have enabled people to grow more food, build large buildings, move objects, animals and people over long distances and make all kinds of things to use. They have made it possible to do work that used to take days or years or even decades in just a short space of time. And they have made the impossible possible.

SUPER MATERIALS

Modern machines use the latest materials – super-strong or light metals, carbon fibres, and light plastics. Some can withstand extremes of temperature, pressure and speed. Some squeeze every last drop of power from their energy source to go further, faster or for longer than ever before. And some are simply monsters – giants that use incredible strength to accomplish tasks that would have been impossible just 100 years ago, such as this huge mining excavator (left).

POWERING UP

In the last 100 years, machines have gone from really useful to extreme. The earliest machines were driven by muscle power, wind or flowing water. Then steam engines were invented and things began to heat up. Soon came machines driven by electricity, by internal combustion engines burning fuels, by rocket power and even nuclear power, such as this submarine (above). Worried about damage to the environment from burning fuels, some designers have turned to making green machines that use sunlight or wind power – but they are nothing like the earliest machines.

This solar-powered aircraft combines the latest power sources and the lightest materials.

TRAVELLING OVER LAND

People mostly live, build and travel around on land, so that's where most of our machines have to work. We use them to move ourselves and our goods about, and they range from the slowest crawlers carrying vast space rockets and launch equipment to the fastest, sleekest, whizziest vehicles.

Some are built to be robust and serviceable, powerful machines that can withstand harsh treatment and conditions. Others are built for elegance and luxury, or for speed. In this chapter, you'll find all kinds of machines, for all kinds of uses, but they all have one thing in common: they are all extremes of their kind. They can handle extreme conditions, they have extreme designs or they are just extremely good fun!

The giant buckets of this enormously powerful excavating machine scoop up tonnes of coal with every turn of the wheel.

LARGEST DUMP TRUCKS

You've probably seen dump trucks on building sites, but those are nothing compared to the monster trucks used at mining sites. These beasts have to move massive amounts of debris hauled from the ground by super-big diggers (see pages 24–25). The dump trucks are so big and heavy that they are not allowed to drive on public roads – their weight would break up the surface. Instead, they are made twice: they are put together and tested, then taken apart and delivered in pieces to where they will be used, and rebuilt.

Eight huge tyres spread the weight of the truck and give it stability. But they still have to carry up to 100,000 kg each when the truck is fully loaded!

BELAZ 75710

The BelAZ model 75710 is the world's largest dump truck: it can carry 450,000 kg of soil or rock. At 350,000 kg, it weighs as much as two blue whales even when it's empty – when it's full, it weighs more than four blue whales! The truck is made in Belarus, but used around the world.

757

The truck is just over 20 m long – nearly as long as two bin lorries.

LIEBHERR T 282 B

The Liebherr T 282 B is a little smaller than the BelAZ, but the deeper truck bed means it can carry a greater volume. It's not built for speed – the fastest it can go fully loaded is 64 km/h. But that's quite fast enough over the rough ground of a mining site. Dump trucks use hydraulics to lift the front part of the carrier and tip out the load.

CATERPILLAR 797F

The Caterpillar 797F can carry loads of 400,000 kg. Its fuel tank holds 7,571 litres of fuel – that's more than a hundred times as much as most cars. Its six 5,300 kg tyres cost more than US$42,000 each – so each tyre costs as much as an expensive family car!

Speediest Motorbikes

Sports motorbikes are the fastest mass-produced motorbikes in the world. In 2000, rumours of a top speed limit being imposed by European law led Japanese and European manufacturers to limit all motorbikes to 300 km/h voluntarily. All bikes from 2000 onwards are electronically limited to this speed – they just can't go any faster.

SUZUKI HAYABUSA

The Suzuki Hayabusa is technically the fastest sports motorbike there will ever be! Released in 1999, just before the 300 km/h limit, it can reach a top speed of up to 312 km/h. As no later motorbike is allowed to go any faster, it will keep its record forever. The name 'Hayabusa' is Japanese for 'peregrine falcon', a bird known for plunging dives at super-high speed. Living up to its name, the Hayabusa can accelerate from 0 to 100 km/h in under three seconds.

The designer of the Hayabusa aimed for a 'grotesque' feel to the design so that it would make a strong impact.

DODGE TOMAHAWK

Is it a motorbike or not? The Dodge Tomahawk has four wheels, but they are paired so close together that they look and act like two super-fat wheels. It was only made as a concept vehicle and it's never been legal on the street. Dodge claims it can reach over 400 km/h and possibly 600 km/h, but it's never been properly tested. They call it a rideable 'sculpture' rather than a real bike.

A lightweight aluminium frame makes the Hayabusa light enough to whizz along at top speeds.

MTT TURBINE SUPERBIKE Y2K

The MTT Turbine Superbike Y2K is powered by a jet engine, which can blast it from 0 to 100 km/h in an eye-watering 1.5 seconds. It's not a production bike, so you can't buy one.

Bio-Inspired Ice Vehicle

Crossing the snow and ice of Antarctica is a real challenge for humans and vehicles alike. With average temperatures as low as -57°C, even fuel can freeze. The *Winston Wong Bio-Inspired Ice Vehicle* (*BIV*) was built to cross Antarctica from the west coast to the South Pole in 2010. It proved that biofuel, which is better for the environment than fossil fuel, can power a vehicle in the most extreme conditions, so there's no reason it can't be used for everyday journeys.

Ski-like blades help the vehicle glide over the ice; wheels would sink into softer snow or get jammed in ruts.

CROSSING THE ICE

The *BIV* can zip over the ice at up to 135 km/h in good conditions, but conditions are not always that great in Antarctica. As the vehicle is light, the two men on the expedition can drag the *BIV* over the ground by hauling it with ropes. Antarctica is a dangerous environment, with hidden crevasses (vast cracks and holes in the ice). The *BIV* has a unique Ice Penetrating Radar (IPR) system that can spot crevasses ahead and avoid them even when they are invisible to the human driver.

SUPPORT VEHICLES

The *BIV* was too small to carry everything the expedition needed and acted as a 'scout' seeking out a safe route for two larger and heavier Science Support Vehicles following behind. These carried equipment and supplies, their six-wheel drive engines giving them maximum traction on the ice.

Low suspension helps the *BIV* deal with *sastrugi* – the frozen ridges and dips in the ice caused by the Antarctic winds.

ECO-FRIENDLY

With an engine usually used in motorcycles, the *BIV* runs on E85 bio-ethanol, an eco-friendly fuel made from corn. The chassis was designed by a Formula One designer working with a polar expert. Moving parts are kept to a minimum as they tend to freeze up in the extreme conditions.

HIGH-SPEED TRAINS

What makes a train go slowly? The same thing as makes it go fast – the wheels! Friction between the wheels and the track limits how fast a train can go, no matter how smooth they both are. The solution is to get rid of the wheels. The Shanghai Maglev train does just that, moving the train along using magnets while it floats 8–12 mm above a guideway. There's no friction with the track as the train only touches the air!

The streamlined shape of the train reduces friction with the air, so as soon as it lifts off the guideway it zips along smoothly.

SHANGHAI MAGLEV

The Shanghai Maglev is the fastest train in the world. Running between Shanghai in southern China and Pudong International Airport, it covers the distance of 30 km in just 7–8 minutes. Its top operating speed over the journey is 431 km/h, but if it had a longer run it could reach 501 km/h.

AVE S 103

In Spain, the AVE S 103 is a new breed of train designed to carry people between cities at super-fast speeds. The trains travel at 350 km/h over an expanding network of very high speed rails in the country. The carriages are modern and comfortable, with rotating, reclining seats fitted with video and music players.

The guideway that supports the weight of the train is made of welded steel and reinforced concrete.

FRECCIAROSSA 1000

The Frecciarossa 1000 is the fastest train in Europe, running at up to 360 km/h and capable of a top speed of 575 km/h. Pulling eight cars, and 200 m long, the Frecciarossa runs between Naples in southern Italy and Milan in the north. It's luxurious, too, being very quiet and having climate control, wifi and onboard monitors for personal computers.

NASA CRAWLER TRANSPORTER

This giant crawler is used to move NASA's spacecraft to the launch sites. It's as wide as a six-lane highway and, carrying a rocket, it is as tall as a skyscraper. The trip of just under 5.5 km takes six hours as it has to go so carefully and slowly.

The crawler and Space Shuttle together weighed a huge 8 million kg.

3 SIDE

MASSIVE EFFORTS

The crawler is controlled from two control cabs located at either end of the vehicle. The Kennedy Space Center has been using the same two crawlers, now nicknamed 'Hans' and 'Franz', since 1965. In their lifetime, they have travelled more than 5,500 km.

SPECIFICATIONS

The NASA Crawler Transporter is as extreme as machines get. At 34.4 m wide and 40 m long, it's a sight to be seen. Two diesel engines drive an electric motor that moves the crawler on belts. Two giant belts at each corner have 57 shoes (456 in total), each nearly 2.3 m tall, 0.5 m wide and weighing almost a tonne. One of the crawlers is being upgraded to carry 8,165,000 kg so that it can move NASA's latest heavy-lift rockets.

The tiny steering wheel is the size of the wheel in a go-kart. Hydraulics enable it to turn the gigantic crawler.

ROAD TRAINS

Road trains are chains of truck trailers pulled by extremely powerful tractor units. They are used in Australia and North America to pull huge loads of cattle, fuel and metal ore across the country.

LINKING TOGETHER

Road trains are linked together with special horseshoe-shaped flat metal plates with a gap for a kingpin to fit into. The kingpin locks in place but can swivel, allowing the road train to drive around bends in the road. The same mechanism is used to link the driving truck and the first trailer.

Road trains are used to transport petroleum or oil to and from petrol stations.

This type of Australian three-trailer truck can be 36–50 m long in total.

BIGGEST HAULING TRUCKS

Australia has the biggest and heaviest road trains in the world. Transporting fuel, livestock and all sorts of goods, the largest road trains are found in the outback regions of Australia, and some remote areas are entirely reliant on them. They can be over 50 m long and weigh nearly 200 tonnes.

ROAD

XHR 534

WIND-POWERED VEHICLES

Concern for the environment is leading more and more vehicle designers to think about renewable energy. Wind-powered vehicles make the most of a renewable source and are built for speed – they can go like the wind!

Made of strong carbon composites, the sail takes powerful side wind force and converts it to movement over the ground.

GREENBIRD

Is it a plane? Is it a sail-boat? Is it a car? It's bits of all three! The *Greenbird* is a land-going vehicle powered by the wind blowing against its tall, fin-like sail. The sail is rigid, like an aeroplane wing, rather than soft like a boat's sail. Its efficient design traps the wind and boosts it to a speed up to 3–5 times faster. It has reached the wind-powered land speed record of 203 km/h and can go over land or ice.

The wide side wings hold the *Greenbird* down to the ground – otherwise, it would be in danger of taking off or falling over.

VENTOMOBILE

This wacky-looking wind-powered machine has a giant propeller stuck on top of a plane-shaped go-kart! Invented by students at Stuttgart University in Germany, it is the first entirely wind-driven racing car. The wind turns the propeller, and its movement is translated into forward movement of the vehicle.

PTEROSAIL TRIKE

The Pterosail trike uses pedal power and wind power together, and it's a production vehicle – you can buy one. It's a lying-down tricycle but with a sail like that on a windsurfing board. Salt flats and beaches are the best place to use it, and if you're feeling lazy, you don't need to pedal at all. As long as there is wind of at least 13 km/h or so, it will blow along on its own.

PTEROSAIL

greenbird

MILLIONAIRE MOTORHOMES

If you've ever been on holiday in a motorhome, it was probably quite cramped, with fold-out beds and no shower. But motorhomes can be as grand as a palace and nearly as big as a real home – if you have enough money.

THE MARCHI MOBILE ELEMMENT PALAZZO

The Marchi Mobile eleMMent Palazzo is the most luxurious motorhome made. It has a kitchen with ice-maker and coffee machine, a lounge with widescreen satellite TV, wifi, a bedroom with a king-size bed and a walk-in rainfall shower. There's even a pop-up roof terrace called the Sky Lounge with its own lighting and cocktail bar.

ENGINEERED FOR TRAVEL

The Palazzo is engineered for travel, with a strong structure, thick, insulated walls and a top speed of nearly 150 km/h. The space-age driving cab has comfortable leather seats that can swivel around, large windows to give a good view of the road and an aviator dashboard just like a plane.

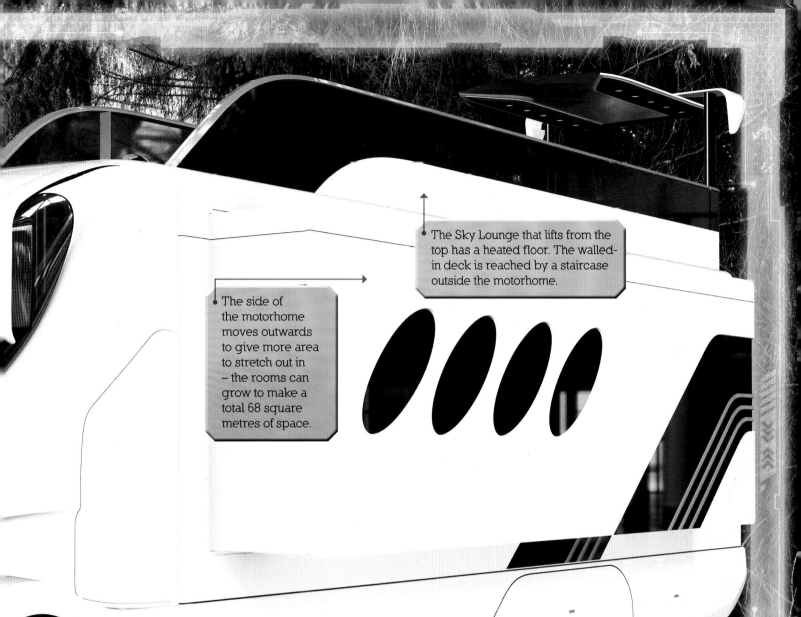

The Sky Lounge that lifts from the top has a heated floor. The walled-in deck is reached by a staircase outside the motorhome.

The side of the motorhome moves outwards to give more area to stretch out in – the rooms can grow to make a total 68 square metres of space.

CARRY YOUR CAR

If you don't quite fancy the Palazzo, the Vantare Platinum Plus is just as luxurious but has slightly different features. There's no sky lounge and the floor doesn't extend, but there's a treadmill with its own screen so you can watch movies while working out. There's even a built-in garage that can carry a small sports car.

Biggest
Diggers

Mining coal and other materials from the ground is tough work and tough machines are needed to do it. Earth and coal are gouged out of the ground by excavators like the massive Bagger 293, the largest movable machine on land.

BUCKET AFTER BUCKET

The Bagger is a bucket wheel excavator. Instead of having one bucket like the diggers you see on building sites, it has a whole series of buckets arranged around a wheel that measures 21 metres across. The Bagger eats its way through the ground, filling its 18 buckets in turn. Each bucket can handle up to 6,800 kg of earth. The buckets drop their load onto a conveyor belt that carries the material along the arm of the excavator and off to other conveyor belts that can carry it far across the mining site.

MINING GIANT

Bagger 293 weighs 14,000,000 kg – as much as about 2,000 elephants. It's as tall as a 30-storey building and at 200 m, as long as two football fields. It's used only at mining sites, so you won't see one on the roads. That's just as well as it moves really slowly – just under 1 km/h.

The arm of the excavator carries the load away from the wheel. An extendable boom on the other side balances the huge machine so it doesn't tip over.

The digger throws up so much fine dust that a constant spray of water is needed to damp it down and keep the dust at safe levels for the operators.

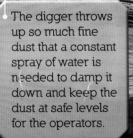

LARGELY AUTOMATED

It takes just five people to operate the Bagger, and with 15 people it can work round the clock in three shifts. Most of the control of the machine is handled automatically, using a system of sensors, GPS (satellite navigation system) and online controls that adjust its activity.

Moving Through THE WATER

Most of the Earth's surface is water, which gives plenty of space for machines that move over, through or under the water. They are used for transport, exploration, scientific investigation, warfare and just fun, and range in size from one-person submersibles to vast ships that cross the oceans or submarines that stay under the sea for months.

Movement in water is slower than movement on land. A land vehicle has to move through air, but a water vehicle has to push through water. The fastest water vehicles move on or above the surface, skimming along with as little of their body in contact with the water as possible. Water exerts more pressure than air, especially deep in the sea, so underwater machines need to be built of tough materials and have strong shapes to keep them from being crushed.

The *Tûranor PlanetSolar* is the world's largest solar-powered boat. It's a trimaran, which means that it has three hulls in order to reduce the amount of the boat's surface in contact with the water.

UNDERWATER GIANTS

Giant submarines can cross the oceans below the water, staying submerged for months at a time. Most are military vessels, patrolling the seas on the look-out for hostile or suspicious activity. They are powered by nuclear reactors onboard. The Russians and the Americans use some of the biggest submarines ever constructed.

The Akula displaces a massive 43,500,000 kg of water when it dives beneath the waves.

RUSSIAN GIANT

The Russian Akula Class submarines, called Typhoon in the west, are the largest ever made. This submarine is 175 m long and has two nuclear reactors. It can sneak quietly along at 50 km/h underwater, or at 41 km/h at the surface. The Akula is crewed by 160 sailors and can stay underwater for 120 days. Six Akula were built in the 1980s, but only one is still in use. The others have been cut into gigantic pieces and recycled.

With three separate pressure hulls, the Akula is wider than any other submarine, but also safer. If one hull is damaged and floods, the others remain secure.

AMERICAN TITAN

The US Ohio Class submarine is smaller than the Akula, displacing only half the volume of water, but it's no less impressive. The biggest submarine in the US Navy, it carries more weapons than the larger sub, and can stay hidden below 250 m of sea for six months at a time, if necessary. It has a crew of 155 officers and sailors, is 170 m long and has a top underwater speed of 46 km/h.

Deep-Sea SUBMERSIBLES

Manned deep-sea submersibles are underwater craft that are used to investigate one of the last unexplored regions on Earth: the bottom of the ocean. These tiny high-tech submersibles have crews of one to three people and are fitted out with vital life-support systems and tough outer shells that can survive the crushing pressure thousands of metres below the surface.

The *Challenger*'s pilot chamber was 1.1 m wide and contained a thruster joystick, a plastic viewing window and three video monitors.

DEEP-SEA CHALLENGER

The *Challenger* is a 7.3 m-long submersible built to reach the world's deepest seabed: the Pacific Ocean's Mariana Trench, 11,000 m below the surface. To protect its owner and pilot, the film director James Cameron, the *Challenger* was fitted with 6.4 cm-thick steel walls, pressure-resistant foam for flotation, and 180 high-tech onboard systems. These systems included lithium batteries, temperature and oxygen controls, LED lighting, 3D cameras and an underwater acoustic communication system.

Ballast weighing 500 kg allowed *Challenger* to sink to the bottom in 2 hours, 37 minutes. After three hours of exploration, the ballast was released to allow the submersible to rise to the surface.

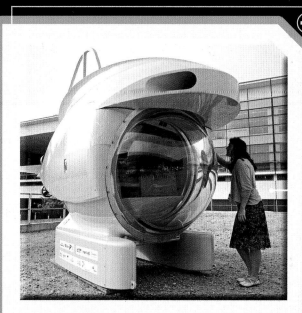

ICTINEU 3

Built with a large front viewing port, electric batteries for propulsion and optional robotic arms, the Spanish *Ictineu 3* submersible is used for industrial work and underwater archaeology. Capable of reaching depths of 1,200 m, the *Ictineu* can carry a pilot and two passengers underwater for up to 10 hours at a time.

JIAOLONG

Designed for geological seabed research, the Chinese *Jiaolong* is only the third submersible to reach a depth of 7,000 m. *Jiaolong* is fitted with sonar systems for communication, anti-collision and imaging, and a high-ballast emergency jettisoning system.

ON LAND AND SEA

Wouldn't it be great if you could ride your bike straight into the water and, instead of it sinking, it skimmed across the waves? Amphibious vehicles do just that – they travel on land using wheels and when they hit the water they transform to water-friendly methods of moving.

BISKI WATER-BIKE

The Biski looks like a motorbike on land, but it converts to a jet ski when it meets water. Taking only five seconds to convert, the wheels rise up into the chassis and two powerful water jets hurl water from the back of the bike. On water it can whizz along at 60 km/h, but on land it goes a lot faster – a respectable 130 km/h.

The rear spoiler rolls down to form the hydrofoil at the back.

RINSPEED SPLASH

The Rinspeed Splash seems like a slightly odd-looking sports car until it hits water.
Then a propeller folds down at the rear and two supports appear at the sides. These raise
the car above the water, converting it to a hydrofoil speedboat that can zip over the water at
80 km/h. The car/boat runs on natural gas and has a motor converted from a snowmobile.
Very sensibly, the interior is all waterproof.

The front hydrofoils
fold out from either
side of the chassis.

HOVERCRAFT

Hovercraft float on a giant cushion of air that carries the craft over land, sea or ice. The inflated 'skirt' is not as squashy as it looks, and gives a bumpy ride. Fans pull air in at the front and push it out at the back, making the craft move forwards. When the hovercraft stops, the skirt deflates, lowering the vehicle so that it's easy for cargo and passengers to get on and off. When it starts up, air is pumped into the skirt, lifting the vehicle.

MORDOVIA

The Russian Zubr-class *Mordovia* is the largest hovercraft in the world – it's also an amphibious attack vehicle. At 57.5 m long and 25.5 m wide, it's more than four buses long and two buses wide. Designed to carry troops and vehicles from ships to land, it has a cruising speed of 55–74 km/h and a top speed of 110 km/h. It can ride waves up to 2.5 m high, and even go over a vertical wall 1.6 m tall!

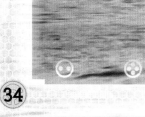

HIVUS-10

The Hivus-10 hovercraft is designed for use on water and on ice, crossing ice-packed sea or frozen tundra. It can be used as a fishing boat, tourist craft or carrier, and also as a rescue vehicle or ambulance. The air cushions are designed so they do not freeze solid and keep the hovercraft manoeuvrable in all conditions.

MERCIER-JONES SUPERCRAFT

The much smaller Mercier-Jones Supercraft is a luxurious sports-hovercraft for just two people. Borrowing design features from luxury cars, it looks like a stylish cross between a speedboat and a sports car. The lightweight, carbon fibre body comes with a comfortable interior, including chilled drinks wells, touch-screen controls, wifi and bluetooth. It can be modified for use over swamps, deserts or the Arctic tundra.

A cargo area of 400 square metres is enough for *Mordovia* to carry three battle tanks or 10 armoured vehicles with 140 soldiers.

With airtight seals and equipment to cloak its own magnetic field so that it doesn't trigger magnetic mines, *Mordovia* is secure against enemy attacks.

FASTEST ON WATER

It's harder to go fast over water than over the ground or through the air – and just as dangerous. But that hasn't stopped the designers of these superfast boats. The fastest compete for the World Unlimited Water Speed Record – first set in 1978 and unbeaten for many years.

The night before his attempt on the world record, Warby cut 6 cm off the rudder to reduce drag and make the boat go faster.

SPIRIT OF AUSTRALIA

Australian Ken Warby built a wooden boat in his backyard. That's not unusual – but his was the fastest boat ever made. He built *Spirit of Australia* using only three power tools, making the rest by hand. It was powered by a jet engine bought from an airforce surplus auction. It produced more than 1,500 kg of thrust, allowing Warby to set a new world record of 511 km/h in 1978.

CIGARETTE AMG ELECTRIC DRIVE

Normally, electricity and water don't mix well, but the Cigarette AMG Electric Drive is an electric powered motorboat that works very well. This concept boat is the most powerful and the fastest electric boat ever designed. It's driven by 12 electric car motors, giving it a top speed of over 160 km/h. As it's electric, it has to be charged before use, but can manage a two-hour trip before it needs re-charging.

The hull was made of plywood and fibreglass over a wooden frame; the tail plane was aluminium.

SAILROCKET 2

Sailrocket 2 smashed the world speed sailing record in 2012 by sailing at 121 km/h. With a structure made of carbon fibre, it's light and strong – which it needs to be as it's hurled over the ocean by the wind. In fact, the boat goes even faster than the wind. Its special design harnesses not just the wind, but also the extra breeze the boat itself makes as it moves. This means the faster it goes, the more wind it generates, which pushes it along even faster.

Monster SHIPS

Huge ships are the only way to move shipments of oil, heavy machinery and mass-produced goods like cars around the world. They are heavy and sluggish. Other ships, such as those used as oil refineries or as storage facilities, are floating platforms that don't move at all. Some are magnificent liners that sail smoothly over the ocean carrying holidaying passengers.

All the storage tanks in the hull can hold as much liquid as 175 Olympic-sized swimming pools.

PRELUDE

Prelude, designed by oil company Shell, is a floating refinery. It processes natural gas taken from the sea, turning it from a gas to a liquid. On board, natural gas is chilled to -162° C, when it turns to liquid. It shrinks to 1/600th of its original volume. *Prelude* will stay moored off the coast of Australia for 25 years, sitting in water that is 250 m deep.

At 488 m long and 74 m wide, *Prelude* is the largest floating vessel in the world – almost as long as five football pitches.

HARMONY OF THE SEAS

The largest passenger ship in the world, *Harmony of the Seas* is just 5 cm longer than her identical sister ship. She's 362 m long and can carry 5,600 passengers in luxurious conditions. On board, people can enjoy a theatre, an ice skating rink, a dance hall, swimming pools, a shopping centre and an outdoor cinema.

PRELUDE

SEAWISE GIANT

The *Seawise Giant*, the largest oil tanker in the world, was sunk off the coast of İraq in 1986 but hauled up years later and rebuilt as the *Jahre Viking*. İt was so enormous it couldn't sail into most of the world's ports or pass through the English Channel, the sea between England and France. The ship was 485 m long and when it was fully loaded it sat 24.6 m deep in the sea, so couldn't enter shallow water. İt stopped sailing in 2010.

GREEN RECORD BREAKER

Shipping uses a huge amount of fuel, so any way of making it more eco-friendly is good news. Some companies are working on using biofuels and even solar energy to power vessels over the sea. It's early days, but maybe one day shipping will become much greener.

The 'horns' are ducts. Hot air from around the engines pours out from them while cold air is sucked in below to cool the engines.

SPEEDY GREEN

Earthrace travelled round the whole world in just 60 days in 2008, a world record for a powerboat. Using eco-friendly biofuel, the journey had a carbon footprint of zero. This made a statement to the world: transport doesn't have to damage the environment. It also used vegetable oil for lubrication and other eco-friendly materials wherever possible. It was still an impressive boat – 24 metres long and an unusual, narrow shape that allowed her to cut through waves in rough seas!

Very narrow hulls allow the boat to slice through waves, rather than riding on top of them like most powerboats.

SOLAR LOON-POWERED BOATS

They are not as zippy as *Earthrace*, but solar loon-powered boats are very eco-friendly. Powered entirely by sunlight falling on the large solar panels on the roof, these passenger boats are great for pleasure trips over inland water. Solar power is stored in batteries, so the boat will still go if there is no sun. The batteries can also be charged from mains electricity if necessary.

A SAD END

Earthrace continued its green career, but it ended in disaster. Renamed MY *Ady Gil*, it was painted black and strengthened with extra carbon fibre and the synthetic material kevlar. It was then used by conservationists in an operation against a Japanese whaling fleet. It was the only boat that could keep up with the fastest whalers. But in 2010, *Ady Gil* was rammed by a whaling vessel and sank.

GETTING OFF THE GROUND

There's more than one way to fly.
Ingenious inventors have made machines that fly in different
ways, from winged aircraft and helicopters with propellers to
jet-propelled backpacks. Flying machines can be used
to carry passengers, lift heavy loads, help out with disaster
relief, visit the edge of space, or just whizz around for fun.

To get airborne, a flying machine needs lift -- the pressure
of air moving around the wings that carries the
machine upwards. A traditional aircraft gains lift
by accelerating on a runway, until the air
underneath pushes it upwards. A helicopter's
whirling rotors force air downwards, so the aircraft
rises up. Once in the air, machines can move using
propellers or rotors that push the air out of the way
to move the vehicle along, or use jet
propulsion. Fuel is burned in an engine and
exhaust gases are forced out of the rear of
the machine, pushing the machine forwards.

The Eurocopter X3 uses a normal horizontal rotor as well as two propeller engines to create a superfast compound helicopter.

Giant PLANES

Since the dawn of aviation, aircraft designers have tried to build bigger and heavier planes. In World War I, multi-engine bombers were developed to deliver heavy payloads hundreds of kilometres away. Later, passenger planes weighing over 50 tonnes showed that pushing gravity to its limits was just as useful during times of peace as those of war.

The *Buran* spacecraft was lifted onto the Antonov An-225 Mriya with huge cranes and fixed into place.

DORNIER DO X

Built in 1929, the German Dornier Do X was an early giant airplane that could carry up to 100 passengers. Weighing a hefty 56 tonnes, the Do X needed 12 engines to fly and was designed to take off and land on water.

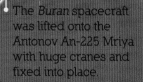

ANTONOV AN-225 MRIYA

Built in 1988 to piggyback the Russian *Buran* space shuttle, the Antonov An-225 is the largest and heaviest aircraft in the world. Known as 'Mriya', the An-225 has 42 wheels, a wingspan of 88.4 m, and six turbofan engines. Today the An-225 carries oversized cargoes around the world, including tanks, wind turbines, power generators, and at one time, 216,000 ready-meals from Germany to a US military base in Oman.

Antonov An-225 holds the record for the highest single payload ever airlifted, at just under 190,000 kg.

AIRBUS A380

First flown in 2005, the Airbus A380 is the largest passenger plane ever built: it has two decks, a wingspan of 79.95 m, a length of 72.72 m and is powered by four turbofan engines. The A380 can carry up to 850 passengers and lift a maximum weight of 575 tonnes.

HEAD-SPINNING HELICOPTERS

Helicopters use fast-spinning rotor blades to create lift. They take off from a standing start and don't need a runway like planes do, and land or take off in little more space than their own footprint. They can also hover for airlifts and drops.

MI-26

The Russian-built Mil Mi-26, also called the Halo, is the world's largest and most powerful helicopter. Its rotor blades measure 32 metres across, giving it the same span as the wings of an Airbus A320. The Mi-26 can carry loads up to about 21,000 kg – as much as 11 family cars. It's been used to transport an airliner slung beneath it, heavy earth-moving equipment to help out in disaster zones, and even a woolly mammoth 23,000 years old, found frozen in the ice of Siberia!

At 40 m long and as tall as a three-storey building, the Mi-26 has plenty of room inside. The huge cargo bay can fit large machinery, 90 passengers or 60 patients on stretchers.

EUROCOPTER X3

The concept Eurocopter X3 is the world's fastest compound helicopter. Unlike a normal helicopter, it uses two large forward-facing propellers as well as a large main rotor to boost its speed. In 2013, it set a world record of 472 km/h.

The rotors and twin engines produce a top speed of 295 km/h, and it cruises at 255 km/h. It can reach an altitude of 4,600 m.

AGUSTAWESTLAND

Helicopters are not usually luxurious, but the AgustaWestland AW101 VIP certainly offers a way to travel in style. With padded leather seats that look like armchairs and enough headroom to stand up and walk around, it's the most comfortable helicopter there is. Intended for carrying VIPs such as presidents, it's also powerful and robust enough for search and rescue missions.

Solar PLANE

Rather than using large amounts of fuel, solar planes harness the power of sunlight. *Solar Impulse 2 (Si2)* is a solar-powered plane that was built to fly around the world. İt achieved this epic journey in 2016.

SLOW MOVER

During the round-the-world trip, *Si2*'s take-off speed was 36 km/h – no faster than a car travelling through town. But the huge wingspan and light weight of the plane gave it enough lift to get off the ground. İts cruising speed was 90 km/h, dropping to 60 km/h to save power at night. İt could reach a maximum speed of 140 km/h if needed. İt took five days to cross the Pacific Ocean, which broke the world record for the longest solo flight by time.

The top surface of the wings, tailplane and fuselage carry 17,248 photovoltaic solar cells giving a total area of 269.5 square metres collecting energy from sunlight.

Si2's cruising height of 8,500 m meant choosing a route to avoid very tall mountains.

A SUNNY START

Si2 was delivered to Abu Dhabi, the United Arab Emirates, by cargo plane. This was the starting point of the journey – a place with lots of sunshine! The solar cells collect energy from sunlight during the day. The energy powers the motors that drive the propellers, and extra is stored in batteries.

A WORLD FIRST

The first round-the-world trip in a solar-powered plane ended in July 2016. The journey of 40,000 km was split into 17 stages. The plane has only one seat, so it had to land to switch between the two pilots who shared the journey. The flight also needed to be planned around good weather and conditions, avoiding monsoon rains and wind and getting maximum sunlight to recharge the solar-cell batteries. The entire trip took more than 16 months and had a support team of 90 people.

SPYPLANES

Planes used by the military focus on stealth and speed. Those used for spying need to be able to whizz past enemy defences without being spotted. They collect images using cameras of different types and intercept enemy signals from the ground and between other craft.

A turbine engine on top of the plane takes it to Mach 3 (three times the speed of sound) and then a more powerful ramjet pushes the speed up to Mach 6.

LOCKHEED SR-72

Still in development, the latest spyplane is the Lockheed SR-72. It's also known as 'Son of the Blackbird' as it's the replacement for SR-71 Blackbird (see page 52). It might be operational by 2030. The hypersonic plane will fly at 7,170 km/h, which is six times the speed of sound, or Mach 6. That's fast enough to get from London to New York in 45 minutes. The plane will be a drone – flown remotely, with no pilot or crew on board.

The Predator first flew in 1995 and is powered by a pusher propeller

PREDATOR

The US spyplane Predator is an unmanned drone. With a 15-m wingspan, Predator flies at a height up to 7,600 m and can stay airborne for 40 hours flying at 130 km/h. It has video and infrared cameras and radar. It is controlled from a mobile ground control station that fits in a trailer measuring just 9 m long. Predator sends the information it collects to the control station, where a pilot flies the plane.

SNEAKY PLANE

The Russian Tu-214R has an extra-sneaky way of going unspotted while collecting data – it's adapted from a normal passenger plane and doesn't look anything like a spyplane! It carries electronic and video surveillance equipment and – although missions are secret – it's known to have been used over Syria in 2016.

Fastest
Jetplane

The fastest plane ever built went from design idea to flight in just 20 months in 1963–4. The Lockheed SR-71, known as the Blackbird, was a revolutionary design. The plan was to make a plane that could fly faster than sound and be impossible to shoot down. No faster plane has ever been built – the Blackbird's top speed was 3,530 km/h, reached in 1976. This is more than three times the speed of sound, so the plane created a loud sonic boom when it sped through the sound barrier at 1,236 km/h.

BLACK AS A BLACKBIRD

Blackbird's name came from its colour, which was used to manage heat. Friction with the air at high speed caused the front edges of the plane to heat up to 537°C. At the same time, other areas were below freezing. Painting the plane black helped to spread the heat evenly over the body. The paint also reduced the plane's ability to reflect radar, helping to keep the plane hidden from the enemy. Blackbird's shape was also specially designed to avoid radar and it succeeded in avoiding enemy fire – it could go faster than the missiles shot at it!

The plane landed at 315 km/h. To help slow it down and protect the tyres, it used parachutes on landing.

ROOM FOR TWO

The Blackbird had two cockpits, one behind the other. The pilot sat in the front cockpit and a Reconnaissance Systems Officer worked the surveillance systems in the rear cockpit.

WRINKLY AND LOOSE

The body of the Blackbird was built of titanium alloy. Titanium was the only metal light enough and strong enough to withstand the very high temperatures. The fuselage panels were ridged so they could expand and contract with the varying temperatures, and not split when cooling down. The plane leaked fuel before take-off, then once it was airborne and warmer, the plane's titanium panels would seal.

To the edge of space AND Back!

The newest suborbital planes can go right to the edge of space but don't go into orbit. Space begins at a height of 100 km above sea level. It takes a powerful aircraft to reach that altitude – most long-distance planes cruise at an altitude of about 10–12 km.

UP AND DOWN

A new winged spacecraft, called SpaceShipTwo, will take six passengers and two crew members to 110 km above Earth. Custom-designed seats that are upright during take-off and reclined when the craft re-enters Earth's atmosphere make the experience of zero G-forces as comfortable as possible. The spacecraft is carried into the air by an aircraft called WhiteKnightTwo.

SpaceShipTwo is powered by hybrid rockets, which combine the best features of both solid-fuel rockets and liquid-fuel rockets to make the flight as safe and efficient as possible.

BLAST-OFF!

At altitude of 15,000 metres, WhiteKnightTwo releases the spaceship, which fires up its powerful rocket engine, pushing it to a speed of more than 4,000 km/h. This will blast SpaceShipTwo to an altitude of about 110 km and into space, where passengers will be able to view the edge of the atmosphere. The pilots will then rotate the spacecraft's two short wings, slowing it down so that it starts to re-enter the atmosphere.

PASSENGERS INTO SPACE

Once back in Earth's atmosphere, SpaceShipTwo is designed to glide back to the ground, taking 25 minutes to descend to its specially built landing strip and spaceport in New Mexico, USA. It will land on the long runway using an undercarriage made up of two sets of wheels and a nose skid that is made from a wood composite. The design of SpaceShipTwo is based on its predecessor, SpaceShipOne, which in 2004 claimed the $10 million Ansari X Prize offered to the first private company to launch a manned reusable spacecraft.

As it glides back down to land, the wings are rotated back down so that they sit horizontally.

JETPACKS

Wouldn't it be fun to be able to fly just by pushing a button on your backpack and zooming up into the air? Jetpacks have been seen in science fiction for years and years, but finally they are real.

The pilot steers the wing by using a hand throttle and their body, allowing them to fly wherever they want to!

JET WINGPACK

The Jet Wingpack is a backpack with a carbon fibre wing spanning about 2.4 m. The backpack contains four small jet engines adapted from model aircraft engines. The pilot jumps out of a plane at a height of about 2,100 m and horizontal flight is enabled thanks to the foldable wings that unfold while in free fall. The Jet Wingpack can soar to 1,200 m and travel at speeds of up to 200 km/h. If it spins out of control the wing unit can be detached from the pilot and the pilot and the wing descend safely to Earth on separate parachutes.

Just before the pilot jumps out of the plane, they start up the engines with the wings folded. The wings unfold while they are in free fall.

MARTIN JETPACK

The Martin Jetpack was initially designed to be used by rapid response units to get to areas that bulky helicopters can't reach, such as near trees or between buildings. It's powered by a petrol engine and two ducted fans and can be flown manned or unmanned. The pilot steers the jetpack using two joysticks next to each hand and it can reach heights of up to 760 m and achieve a speed of about 40 km/h.

FROM FICTION TO FACT

Jetpacks first appeared in sci-fi comics of the 1920s – and they were so appealing that people wanted to build them. In 1969, the American Bell Aerosystems company produced the Jet Flying Belt that used a single turbofan jet engine. Its first flight was about 100 m at a height of just 7 m, reaching a speed of 45 km/h. Sadly, the US army would not fund its development, so the idea never took off properly.

MACHINES THAT STAY STILL

Not all machines move around. Some are so large they are built in one place and stay there, or have to be moved by other large vehicles to where they will be used. Cable car systems are fixed in place, often stretching all the way up the side of a steep mountain or over a deep gorge. They have moving cars hung from a cable to carry people up and down. Roller coasters have moving 'trains' to give people a fun ride at very high speeds – but the structure is fixed.

Other machines carry out mechanical tasks, such as lifting huge loads or boring tunnels under the ground or through mountains. The largest machine in the entire world is in an underground tunnel and used for research into the tiniest particles, much smaller than atoms.

Formula Rossa in Abu Dhabi is the fastest roller coaster in the world. The track is 2.2 km long and the cars reach speeds of nearly 240 km/h.

HIGH-CLIMBING CABLE CARS

Cable cars are often used to go up mountains or span valleys where it would be very expensive and difficult to build roads. The compartments, called 'cars' or 'gondolas', hang from a cable and are paired, so that while one goes up another goes down.

PEAK 2 PEAK GONDOLA

The Peak 2 Peak Gondola in Canada stretches between two mountain peaks, Whistler and Blackcomb. It allows skiers to ski on both mountains without going down to the valley and back up. At its highest, it's a world record-breaking 436 m above the valley floor – that's a breathtaking drop to see beneath your feet, and two of the cars have glass floors!

In each direction there are two guide cables, which don't move, and a single haul rope, which pulls the gondolas along. The cables total 26.5 km in length.

TELEFERICO DE MERIDA

The Teleférico de Mérida in Venezuela climbs from the city of Mérida to the Pico Espejo, over a distance of 12.5 km. It is the second-longest cable car in the world, but works at much higher altitude than any other. The Mérida end is 1,640 m above sea level and the final destination on Pico Espejo is 4,765 m above sea level. Four cars operate at a time, each able to hold 36 passengers, swinging high above the rugged mountain scrubland below.

HUASHAN CABLEWAY

Mount Huashan in Shaanxi is one of the steepest mountains in China, so climbing it is hard work. Luckily, the Huashan cable car offers another way up to the North peak. But it's one of the scariest and most thrilling rides in the world. The small gondolas, each holding just six passengers, swing over a huge drop. It takes six nail-biting minutes to complete the trip.

The Peak 2 Peak ride in Canada is 4.4 km long. It has the longest single span of cable without a support tower in the world, at 3.03 km.

Big BORERS

Have you ever wondered how tunnels are built? They are drilled out of the ground by giant borers. These monsters move slowly underground, eating through the soil and rock and pushing it backwards out of the way.

BERTHA AND MARTINA

The two largest boring machines in the world are called Bertha and Martina. Bertha is used to dig through soft ground (soil) and Martina through hard ground (rock). At the front of the borer, a rotating cutting plate slices or chips away soil or rock. This falls inside the front of the borer and is carried away on a conveyor belt to be lifted out of the tunnel. As the tunnel gets longer, the conveyor belt coming out the back to remove the muck has to get longer too.

The cutterhead is 17 m across and puts 40 million kg of pressure on the soil in front of it. Bertha gnaws through enough soil to move forward about 10 m a day.

As the borer eats its way through the ground, it builds a tunnel lining from curved sections of concrete. These support the newly dug tunnel.

TRAILING BEHIND

The whole machine is 99 m long and weighs 6,350,000 kg. Around 90 m of its length is to support machinery. This section contains all the supplies, such as concrete sections for the lining and the grout to fix them together, and all the facilities needed by the crew of 25.

MOUNTAIN SLICER

The very first machine for digging tunnels was called the Mountain Slicer. İt was built to cut a tunnel through the Alps, the mountains between France and İtaly.
İt consisted of 100 percussion drills mounted on the front of a machine the size of a locomotive train and mechanically driven into the rock. Unfortunately, the European revolutions of 1848 interrupted work and the tunnel was built 10 years later using ordinary tools.

RECORD ROLLER COASTERS

Do you like thrills? Do you like to go really fast and hurtle along in a tiny truck at eye-popping speeds feeling sick and exhilarated? If so, these record-breaking roller coasters are for you. If you can't visit them, there are POV (point of view) videos on YouTube Kids, so you can see just what it's like to ride them.

Each open-air train holds 24 passengers and there are three trains, giving enough capacity for 1,200 passengers an hour.

The track is 1,041 m long, made of 103 pieces held up by 51 supports. The heaviest single piece of track weighs 7,700 kg.

VALRAVN

The tallest, fastest, longest roller coaster is Valravn at Cedar Point, Ohio, USA. The ride starts with a steep climb to 68 m. There, the floorless compartments freeze suspended over the vertical drop for four long, terrifying seconds. Then they plunge straight down, reaching 120 km/h before climbing the next hill and plunging again. The ride is named after a mythological bird in Danish folklore called Valravn, meaning 'raven of the slain'.

FORMULA ROSSA

Formula Rossa at Ferrari World in Abu Dhabi, United Arab Emirates, is the fastest roller coaster in the world. The ride is based on Formula One and it reaches 240 km/h in under five seconds – faster acceleration than a Formula One racing car! The track is 2.2 km long, its shape inspired by the Italian racetrack Autodromo Nazionale Monza.

KINGDA KA

Kingda Ka at Six Flags Great Adventure in Jackson, USA, is tiger-themed and ferociously scary! It's the tallest roller coaster in the world, and the second fastest. The trains climb to a height of 139 m and then hurtle down, reaching 206 km/h in just 3.5 seconds.

INCREDIBLE CRANES

Cranes are used to lift heavy or large objects, but there are lots of different types. You have probably seen cranes at work in building sites and perhaps dockyards, but you are unlikely to have seen any as extreme as these.

TAISUN STATIC CRANE

The Taisun static crane is used in the Yantai Raffles Shipyard in Shandong Province, China. The Taisun is a gantry crane – a rectangular frame that lifts a load in the space between its two supports. It is used to install very large parts onto semi-submersibles, like drilling platforms and ships. The crane lifts the part, then the hull is lined up under the frame and the part is lowered into place.

The crane spans a gap of 120 m and is 122 m tall and 130 m long.

LIEBHERR LTM 11200-9.1

Liebherr LTM 11200-9.1 is the most powerful mobile crane in the world. It also has the longest telescopic boom ever made, extending to 100 m. Mobile cranes can't lift as much as static cranes, but this monster can still lift up to 1,200,000 kg – the weight of nearly 700 cars! It is supported by nine pairs of wheels, and extendable supports stop the crane falling over when the boom is extended.

Taisun can lift a load of 20,000,000 kg up to a height of 70 metres.

THIALF

Thialf is a crane vessel – a shipping vessel that is moored during use. This monster is fitted with two cranes and can lift 14,200,000 kg. It is used to install foundations and pylons rooted under the water. It can lift loads 95 m high and carry them down to 460 m below deck height. People work for a long time on this crane, and there is living space for 736 people. It even has its own helicopter pad!

LARGEST MACHINE IN THE WORLD

The largest machine ever built is the Large Hadron Collider (LHC) in Geneva, Switzerland. It is a giant underground tunnel, built in a loop to make a complete circle that is 27 km long. It is a particle accelerator – a device that makes particles smaller than atoms travel at extremely high speed. Particles called protons are accelerated and then smashed together so that scientists can see what is produced in the collision.

Particles are sent in bunches of around 115 billion at a time. With 230 billion all entering the collision space at the same time, there is a good chance of collisions.

CIRCULAR PATHS

Particles are accelerated around two separate circular paths going in opposite directions, side by side. There are four intersection points where the particle beams can come together and collide. A series of superconducting magnets, cooled to -271.3°C by liquid helium, keep the beams on the right path.

FASTER THAN FAST

The accelerated particles travel at just 3 m a second below the speed of light. They complete a circuit of the full 27-km tunnel in just 90 millionths of a second. That means a proton travels all the way around the collider 11,000 times in a second.

CALCULATING RESULTS

The LHC is used by scientists to test theories in high level physics, some relating to particles created in the first moments of the universe. So much data is produced by the LHC that the largest computing grid in the world is used to process it, covering 170 computer facilities in 36 countries.

1,232 magnets keep the beams moving in a circle. Another 392 magnets direct the beams at collision points to increase the chance of collisions.

Travelling About In Space

Machines are no longer stuck on Earth but can zoom off into space. They give us a way of exploring space safely by sending information and pictures back to Earth, and of carrying humans into space. We have sent machines further into space than any people have ever been. The first machines ever to go into space were rockets that briefly went beyond the boundary of space – 100 km above sea level – and then returned to Earth. Fewer than 100 years later, we can now send spacecraft to distant planets and moons. Machines can survive conditions no human could live in: extreme heat and cold, extreme pressure, acidic and poisonous fumes and extreme gravity. Space exploration really does need extreme machines!

The Lunar Roving Vehicle was carried to the Moon on board the last three Apollo missions. It was designed to carry astronauts around the lunar surface so they could explore a greater area.

Reusable
Rockets

Not everything that goes into space can fly on its own. Most satellites and spacecraft are launched by rockets that then fall away and are destroyed, but that's an expensive way to work. The latest rockets use vertical take-off, vertical landing (VTVL) techniques, so they can land safely and be re-used.

A single engine in the second stage burns for up to 397 seconds to push a payload into the right orbit. It can be started and stopped to deliver several payloads into different orbits.

INSIDE THE DRAGON

The *Dragon* capsule, which is launched into space by the VTVL rocket *SpaceX Falcon 9*, is a fully functioning spacecraft with its own thrusters and navigation system. It has a pressurised capsule and unpressurised trunk for carrying payloads. In the future, it will carry astronauts and larger payloads can go in an alternative structure on top of the *Dragon*, which at 13 m is long enough to hold a bus.

The *Dragon* is 8 m long and 3.7 m across. With a full payload, it weighs 6,000 kg.

FALCON 9 FULL THRUST

The *SpaceX Falcon 9* is the first-ever reusable rocket. It is used to launch satellites and deliver equipment to the International Space Station. It starts in the same way as traditional rockets: nine thrust engines in the first stage of the rocket burn for 162 seconds to blast *Falcon 9* into space. But unlike previous launchers, *Falcon 9*'s first stage returns to Earth, landing safely on a drone ship in a manoeuvre that looks rather like a reverse blast-off!

NEW SHEPARD

Blue Origin's spacecraft *New Shepard* aims to take passengers into space using a reusable launcher. The passenger capsule sits on top of a VTVL rocket launcher. It was the first booster rocket ever to make a soft landing when it returned from a launch in 2015. Blue Origin aims to start passenger flights in 2018.

Probes and Orbiters

Most machines that go into space don't carry people at all. They are controlled from Earth as they explore distant space. These are probes and orbiters that fly past, orbit or even land on other planets and moons, collecting data, samples and photographs to send back to Earth.

INTO THE UNKNOWN

Only one human-made object has ever left the solar system: the probe *Voyager 1*, launched in 1977. Because it's so old, it is simple by modern standards. But its course set for deep space has already taken it further than any other machine has ever gone. During its mission it flew past the giant planets of Jupiter and Saturn, as well as Saturn's moon, Titan. It officially left the solar system in August 2012 and will never come back; it's already more than 20 billion km from Earth and still going!

Voyager's maximum speed is 62,140 km/h – or 17 km a second. That's the fastest speed of any spacecraft. It will run out of nuclear fuel in 2025, but could carry on travelling for thousands of years as there is nothing to slow it down.

HELLO ALIENS!

Voyager 1 carries a 'golden record' intended for any aliens that find it. The record includes photographs of plants, animals (including humans) and landscapes on Earth, sounds, including greetings in many languages, and information about Earth and its location. *Voyager* will approach another star in 40,000 years, although it won't go very close. But if any aliens have extreme technology of their own, they might find it.

Voyager 1 is so far away that radio signals from Earth take more than 16 hours to reach it – even though radio signals travel at the speed of light.

JUNO ORBITER

NASA's *Juno* orbiter arrived at the planet Jupiter in 2016 on a mission to photograph and investigate Jupiter and its many moons. It took 20 months to reach Jupiter. The solar-powered orbiter has three large solar panels. As it travels, it spins around, its instruments sweeping across a wide field of view to collect as much information as possible. It whirls around three times a minute, making 400 turns in the two hours it takes to travel between Jupiter's north and south poles.

SPACE LANDERS AND ROVERS

While orbiters and probes stay in space to take readings and photographs, rovers land on a planet or moon and collect data, samples and pictures from the surface. So far, rovers have visited the Moon and Mars, and a tiny lander has even dropped onto a comet.

YUTU

Yutu, which means 'jade rabbit', was the first rover to land on the Moon in 40 years when it arrived in 2013. *Yutu* was programmed to hibernate, or shut down most of its systems, during the freezing 14-day night on the Moon.

Yutu 2 landed on the far side of the Moon in January 2019. One of *Yutu 2*'s missions is to explore a massive crater called the Aitken Basin, which is about 13 km deep.

Weighing nearly 180 kg – as much as two fridges – each rover had instruments to investigate the rocks, soil and dust on Mars and carried special tools to dig below the surface.

PHILAE

The lander *Philae* bounced several times when attempting the first 'soft' landing on a comet. Launched on the European spaceship *Rosetta* in 2004, *Philae* took 10 years to reach comet 67P/Churyumov–Gerasimenko. Just 1 m across and 80 cm tall, *Philae* sent back photos and data about what the comet is made of, but lost contact with Earth part way through its mission.

Each rover landed in a spacecraft slowed by parachutes, rockets fired downwards and airbags. The spacecraft then opened like petals on a flower so the rover could roll off its platform and explore.

MARS EXPLORATION ROVER

The Mars Exploration Rovers, named *Spirit* and *Opportunity*, were launched by NASA in 2003 and landed on Mars six months later. Each rover had six wheels, which allowed them to move in many directions. Signals were sent back to scientists, who told the rovers what to do from Earth.

INTERNATIONAL SPACE STATION

The International Space Station (ISS) is the largest-ever habitable space station – a complex of living spaces, equipment, research laboratories and docking areas for visiting spacecraft. It orbits the Earth at an altitude of 330–435 km, taking 93 minutes to make a full orbit.

The robotic arm assembly is 16.7 m long and can lift 100,000 kg – the weight of a space shuttle.

SCIENCE IN SPACE

Staff on the space station visit for months at a time. They maintain the space station and carry out experiments and research. Scientists on ISS work on many areas, including astronomy; space medicine and how the human body responds to conditions in space; the effects of microgravity and space conditions on animals, plants and materials; and weather in space and on Earth. They collaborate with scientists on Earth and with students and school pupils.

BUILT IN SPACE

The entire International Space Station weighs as much as 320 cars and is the size of a football pitch. It's so large that it had to be built in space – nothing could launch something so big into space. It took 115 space flights to deliver all the parts and build the space station. Work started in 1998 and the ISS has been inhabited by astronauts constantly since 2000, breaking the record for continuous use of a space station.

The solar panels are 73 m across in total – as large as the wingspan of a jumbo jet. They provide energy from the Sun to power the space station.

YOU CAN SEE IT!

The ISS is so large it can be seen from Earth, glowing with reflected sunlight. Its location can be found on NASA's website and it is best viewed near sunset or sunrise. It's not visible in daylight, and in the middle of the night it is in the shadow of Earth.

GLOSSARY

BIOFUEL Fuel made from plant material or animal waste rather than fossil fuels such as gas, coal and petrol.

CARBON FIBRE A very thin, long strand of the element carbon.

CHASSIS The framework on which a vehicle is built; it usually sits under the body of the vehicle.

DRY DOCK A space that can be flooded with water to float a ship and then drained, allowing people to work on the ship supported on a platform.

FRICTION A force that operates between two surfaces in contact, or one surface and the air or water, causing resistance to movement.

FUSELAGE The main body of a plane, usually tube-shaped.

GPS Global Positioning System. A global navigation system that provides information about location and time using beams bounced between the object on Earth and satellites in orbit above Earth.

HULL The main body of a ship or boat.

HYDRAULIC Using the force of moving or compressed liquids.

HYDROFOIL A boat that is lifted out of the water, resting on two shaped vanes (also called hydrofoils), so that it travels quickly over the water.

INTERNAL COMBUSTION ENGINE An engine that works by setting fire to liquid fuel in a contained space, making a small explosion that forces a piston (rod-shaped plug) to move along a cylinder. The movement of the piston is used to drive the engine.

LUBRICATION Easing movement by adding a layer of something slippery, such as oil or grease, between two surfaces allowing them to slide over each other smoothly.

NAVIGATION Plotting and following a course of travel.

NOZZLE An opening at the end of a tube through which liquid or gas flows.

NUCLEAR FUEL Chemical element with unstable atoms which can be forced to change, releasing large amounts of energy.

ORBIT The circular path of one body around another, such as the Moon around the Earth. An object in orbit stays a fixed distance away from the body it is orbiting.

PHOTOVOLTAIC Able to convert energy from sunlight into electricity.

PYLON A tall structure like a tower, used to carry cables or as a support for a structure such as a bridge.

RADAR A system that uses radio waves to detect the presence and movement of objects. The radio waves bounce off an object and their reflection is measured to gather information about the shape and location of the object.

RUDDER A movable flat panel at the back of a boat or plane, used for steering the vehicle.

SONIC BOOM The bang created by an object or vehicle breaking the sound barrier – achieving a speed faster than the speed of sound (340 metres per second in air at 20 °C).

SPECTROMETER A piece of equipment for measuring the intensity, or wavelength and frequency, of light.

SUBMERSIBLE A small vehicle that can be used underwater, often for research. Unlike a submarine, it needs the support of a larger vessel at the surface.

SUPERCONDUCTING MAGNET An electromagnet produces a magnetic field by passing electricity through a metal coil. A superconducting magnet is chilled to a very low temperature to conduct extra electricity and so produces a stronger magnetic field.

SURVEILLANCE The activity of keeping watch on a person or group, often secretly.

TELESCOPIC Capable of extending and contracting in length by having one part of a tube sliding into or out of another.

THRUST The force that pushes a vehicle forward, produced by a rocket or jet engine.

TUNDRA Very cold area of land where no trees grow and plants are stunted by cold and often dry conditions.

TURBINE A machine for producing movement from a wheel turned by the action of water, gas or steam.

ACKNOWLEDGEMENTS

The publishers would like to thank the following sources for their kind permission to reproduce the pictures in this book. The page numbers for each of the photographs are listed below, giving the page on which they appear in the book and any location indicator (T-top, B-bottom, L-left, R-right).

AFP: /Samsung Heavy Industries: 38-39
Aerohod Ltd.: 35TL
Alamy: /Mark Chivers/robertharding: 54L; /Simon Critchley: 18-19; /EPA: 56-57; /Ali Haider/EPA: 56R; /Keystone Pictures USA: 36-37, 36BL; /Geof Kirby: 39BR; /Sputnik: 44-45; /Robin Townsend/EPA: 31TR; /Fabian von Poser/imageBROKER: 58-59
Blue Origin: 73BR
CERN: /Maximilien Brice: 68-69
Cedar Point: 64-65
Cigarette Racing Team, LLC: 37TR
Dreamstime: /Grantotufo: 68BL; /photo360: 45B
Earthrace: 40-41, 40BL
Featherlite Coaches: 23BR
Getty Images: /AndrTs Ceballos Arenas: 15TR; /Bettmann: 29BR, 44BL; /Bloomberg: 9R; /China Photos: 61BR; /Christopher Deahr: 9TR; /Georges DeKeerle/Sygma: 28-29; /Krzysztof Dydynski: 61TL; /Lionel Flusin/Gamma-Rapho: 32-33; /Iain Masterson: 65TL; /Joe McNally: 65BR; /Francis Miller/The LIFE Picture Collection: 57BR; /Bryan Mitchell: 11TR; /Peter Parks/AFP: 76L; /Eliot J. Schechter: 17TR; /Stocktrek Images: 5T; /Visual China Group: 31BR, 57TL; /Phil Walter: 41BR
Gibbs Amphibians Ltd.: /Chris McLennan: 32BL
Greenbird: 20-21
Jafafa Hots: 21R
Institute of Aircraft Design, University of Stuttgart: /Inventus: 21T
iStockphoto: /Joe Lena: 50-51; /miralex: 67B; /Nikada: 14-15; /stockstudioX: 60-61; /Leit Wolf: 8-9
Liebherr: 67T
Lockheed Martin: 50B, 52-53, 52B, 53R
Marchi Mobile: 22-23
Marine Turbine Technologies, LLC: 11BR
MARS Scientific: 55TR
Mercier-Jones: 35BR
Moon-Regan Trans Antarctic Expedition: 12-13, 13TR, 13BR
NASA: 16-17, 70-71, 73T, 74-75, 75BL, 78-79, 78BL, 79TR, 79B; /ISS: 72-73; /JPL: 75TR, 77T; /JPL/Cornell University, Maas Digital LLC: 76-77; /Kim Shiflett: 16BL
RWE Power AG: 24-25, 24L, 25BR
Rex/Shutterstock: /KeystoneUSA-ZUMA: 30-31
Rinspeed AG: 33TR
Sailrocket: /Helena Darvelid: 37B
Shutterstock: /Fingerhut: 42-43; /ID1974: 34-35; /Igor Karasi: 26-27; /Andrey Khachatryan: 47BR; /Sergey Kohl: 47TL; /Mik Lav: 4BL; /David Maska: 6-7; /Kevin Norris: 18BL; /Polonio Video: 15BR; /vaalaa: 46-47; /xdrew: 69TR
Solar Impulse: /Pizzolante: 48L; /Revillard/Rezo.ch: 48-49; /Stefatou/Rezo.ch: 4-5
Suzuki: 10-11
Virgin Galactic: /Mark Greenberg: 54-55
Washington State Department of Transportation: 62-63, 63T
Wikimedia Commons: /Daniel Christensen: 39TL; /Haakman: 66-67; /Rimma Sadykova: 51BR

Every effort has been made to acknowledge correctly and contact the source and/or copyright holder of each picture and Carlton Books Limited apologises for any unintentional errors or omissions that will be corrected in future editions of this book.